GW00726863

HISS THE VILLAIN

HISS THE VILLAIN

or

FOILED and COUNTERFOILED

A Melodrama in One Act

Adapted from *The Poor of New York*

by

A. R. TAYLOR

and

W. ERNEST COSSONS

SAMUEL FRENCH

FRENCH

LONDON
NEW YORK TORONTO SYDNEY HOLLYWOOD

822 TAY

BF89962

© 1952 BY SAMUEL FRENCH LTD

This play is fully protected under the copyright laws of the British Commonwealth of Nations, the United States of America, and all countries of the Berne and Universal Copyright Conventions.

All rights are strictly reserved.

It is an infringement of the copyright to give any public performance or reading of this play either in its entirety or in the form of excerpts without the prior consent of the copyright owners. No part of this publication may be transmitted, stored in a retrieval system, or reproduced in any form or by any means, electronic, mechanical, photocopying, manuscript, typescript, recording, or otherwise, without the prior permission of the copyright owners.

SAMUEL FRENCH LTD, 26 SOUTHAMPTON STREET, STRAND, LONDON, WC2, or their authorized agents, issue licences to amateurs to give performances of this play on payment of a fee. **The fee must be paid, and the licence obtained, before a performance is given.**

Licences are issued subject to the understanding that it shall be made clear in all advertising matter that the audience will witness an amateur performance; and that the names of the authors of plays shall be included in all announcements and on all programmes.

The royalty fee indicated below is subject to contract and subject to variation at the sole discretion of Samuel French Ltd.

Fee for each and every
performance by amateurs   15s
in the British Isles

In territories overseas the fee quoted above may not apply. A quotation will be given upon application to the authorized agents, or direct to Samuel French Ltd.

MADE AND PRINTED IN GREAT BRITAIN BY
LATIMER TREND AND CO. LTD, PLYMOUTH
MADE IN ENGLAND

GB 573 02099 X

From 1st September 1972 the fee quoted in this copy for performance by amateurs in the British Isles is increased in accordance with our new scale, copies of which are available from us or from our authorized agents

Samuel French Ltd

CHARACTERS

SILAS SNAKER, *a rascally banker*
BOWLER, *his clerk*
CAPTAIN NOBLE, *an old sea captain*
MRS NOBLE, *his wife*
LUCY, *their daughter*
PERCY, *their son*
HAROLD, *their friend*

SYNOPSIS OF SCENES

SCENE 1: *The Office of Silas Snaker*

SCENE 2: *The Thames Embankment*

SCENE 3: *The Attics in Cross Keys Street*

HISS THE VILLAIN

SCENE 1

SCENE: SNAKER'S *office. The scene can be played in front of a backcloth representing an office, or curtains. Up* C. *is a Victorian desk and stool. Up* R. *is a safe. By the safe is a portmanteau.*

Before the play begins, sinister music is heard.

When the CURTAIN *rises the stage is empty. After a moment,* SNAKER *enters* L. *He is followed by a green spotlight as he advances to the front of the stage. When he speaks the music fades.*

SNAKER. Fortune favours the brave! An hour ago I was a bankrupt. Every stock in which I invested is down. My last effort to retrieve my fortune had plunged me into utter ruin. Tomorrow the streets of London, now so still, would have been filled with a howling multitude. The house of Snaker—the great, respected house of Snaker, the banker—would have fallen, and in falling would crush the hundreds, the thousands of simple folk who have entrusted their pitiful savings to me.

(There are boos.)

And with it would have gone my darling daughter, my innocent, my motherless Alice, but for one stroke of fortune. Just as I was about to bid farewell to the scene of my triumphs and my failure, and to escape, disguised as a musician, in comes a simple old sailor,

1

Captain Noble, in his hands ten thousand pounds in gold. He hands them over to me for safe keeping before he departed on a long voyage, so that in the event of his not returning, his wife and his two children might be safe. Poor trusting fool! Poor trusting fool! Yet, why should I pity him? With his ten thousand pounds I can start afresh.

(*There are boos.*)

I can make *my* child, my Alice, safe from want. Noble's children must starve if need be. *Mine* will be safe.

(*There are boos.* BOWLER *enters* L.)

(*Aside.*) Here is Bowler, my clerk. What the devil do you want?

BOWLER. Captain Noble, the gentleman who was here just now, wishes to see you again, Mr Snaker.

SNAKER. Tell him I've gone. Tell him . . .

(CAPTAIN NOBLE *bursts in* L. *He is a white-whiskered old seaman, though by his gestures he is more of an old actor.*)

NOBLE. Give me back my money, my ten thousand pounds. Give it back, I say. You are a villain, a thief, a swindler.

(*There are cheers.*)

Give me my money. Five minutes after leaving your office I heard rumours that your credit had been shaken by the slump on Wall Street. Then I heard that—never mind what I heard. Enough that you would have taken my money and robbed my innocent children—my darling Percy, my sweet Lucy.

SNAKER. But this is preposterous, sir! What money?

NOBLE. Ten thousand pounds in solid gold. You have it in that safe. I saw you place it there. I and your clerk here saw you. (*To* BOWLER.) Did you not? (*Taking a paper from his pocket.*) And here is your receipt.

(SNAKER *looks anxious.*)

BOWLER (*snatching the receipt*). I saw nothing. I heard you speak of ten thousand pounds, but we get lots of crazy folk here.

NOBLE. Crazy! Merciful heavens! Crazy I shall be unless you . . . (*He grabs vainly at the receipt.*)

BOWLER. Crazy folks who babble about fortunes that don't exist. You go home quietly to your friends.

NOBLE. So you're in this swindle too, this conspiracy. (*He produces a pistol.*) Open that safe and give me my money, or I fire.

(*There are cheers.*)

SNAKER. Seize him!

(BOWLER *struggles with* NOBLE *and wrests the pistol from him.* SNAKER *remains calm, twisting his moustachios in cynical indifference.*)

Now, after this exhibition, will you kindly go, or shall I call the police?

NOBLE. The pol—— (*He struggles from* BOWLER'S *grasp.*) You infernal pair of swindlers. I . . . (*He is overcome by emotion and falls dead.*)

BOWLER (*stooping over* NOBLE *and feeling his heart*). Dead!

(*There are boos.*)

SNAKER. Good! Now, Bowler, do as I tell you. Outside there is a thick fog. We must deposit the body where it will be found in due course. There is nothing about it to contradict the obvious surmise that this man died a perfectly natural death.

BOWLER.   And then?

SNAKER.   I don't understand you.

BOWLER.   What do you take me for?   What do I get out of this?

SNAKER.   Do this and keep your mouth shut, and I will give you—five pounds.

BOWLER.   Fivepence!   Five thousand pounds! Half-shares and no monkey tricks.

SNAKER.   You are mad.

BOWLER.   Mad!   Don't forget I hold all the cards. Only I know about the fortune in that safe.   Think of the story I can tell the police.   I have the receipt——

SNAKER.   Aha!

BOWLER.   —and the pistol.   (*He produces the pistol.*)   Hand over half the money, or . . .

SNAKER.   Foiled!   Curse it!

(*There are cheers.*)

(*He goes slowly to the safe and takes out a bag of gold.*)   Take one thousand.

BOWLER.   Five thousand.

SNAKER.   Take one thousand and spare me.   Think of my innocent che-ild.

BOWLER.   Think of Noble's receipt.   Count your-self lucky that I do not demand the whole ten thousand. Think of the receipt.   With this I could weave a rope that will . . .   (*Still keeping* SNAKER *covered, he makes a significant gesture.*)

SNAKER.   Foiled again!   Curse you, curse you, curse you!   (*Pleading.*)   Do not be hard on a poor man.   Think of my darling Alice, my only, my sweet, my innocent child.

BOWLER.   Quick.   The money, or I take the receipt and vanish.

SNAKER.   Foiled again!   Very well——   (*He opens the safe and flings five money bags on the desk.*)   Keep your paltry scrap of paper, and much good may it do you.   (*Aside.*)   I will find a means yet to thwart him.

(*There are boos.*)

BOWLER (*putting the money bags into the portmanteau*). And now farewell, Silas Snaker. We shall meet again. (*Still keeping* SNAKER *covered, he goes to the door* L.)

SNAKER. But, Bowler, what about the body?

BOWLER. Oh, I don't want it. Do what you like with it. Tip it out of the window. Lock it up in the safe. It's no use to me. Faaaaaaaaaaaaarewellllllllllll!

(BOWLER *exits* L.)

SNAKER. Foiled again!

(*There are prolonged boos and hisses.*)

CURTAIN

MISS THE VILLAIN!

SCENE 2

SCENE: *The Thames Embankment. This scene can be played in front of a backcloth or curtains. There is a bench* L. *and a bench* R.

When the CURTAIN *rises the stage is in darkness except for spotlights on the two benches. Tragical music is played. Big Ben chimes; the wind blows, and snow falls. On the* R. *bench* MRS NOBLE *and* LUCY *sit clasped in each other's arms. On the* L. *bench* BOWLER *is huddled up asleep.* MRS NOBLE *is weeping.*

LUCY. Do not cry, dear mother. (*She produces a handkerchief.*) Come, wipe your unhappy eyes that gaze so sadly on the past.

MRS NOBLE. Nay, Lucy, my darling daughter, I do not weep because of the past. I have long since ceased to show my sorrow for the death of your dear father, though Heaven knows how sadly I still miss the sound of his feet and his merry laughter.

LUCY. It is five years today since he died so suddenly in that pitiless fog. Oh! Cruel fate that thus robbed me of the kindliest father I ever had. (*She produces another handkerchief and sobs.*)

MRS NOBLE. Do not cry, dear daughter. Your father, Captain Noble, was a brave man, so let your tears be turned to smiles of pride. But alas, alas, that he should have left us so unprovided for. I cannot believe that he squandered his money. Some villainous thief stole it from him. He had, I know, ten bags each filled with gold which he took away the night he left us for ever. (*She sobs.*)

LUCY. Do not cry, dear mother. I am so hungry. And so must you be, for we have not eaten for three weary weeks.

6

MRS NOBLE. Patience, darling, patience. **Your** brother, Percy, will be here at any moment. **He is** walking the streets in search of food.

LUCY. Ah, my brave and handsome brother, how I long to help him. Mother, why will you not let me walk the streets, too?

MRS NOBLE (*rising*). Hush, hush, my child. (*Aside.*) She is so innocent. You may walk a few steps to see if he is coming, but do not go out of sight. I want you at my side.

LUCY (*rising and looking* L.). Mother, darling, here is Percy returning. Alas, his hands are empty. But stay, he has a companion. Saved! Saved! Percy has found a friend to help us in our destitution.

(*There are cheers. Music is played as* PERCY *and* HAROLD *enter* L.)

PERCY. Mother! Lucy! See whom I have found. Harold Headingford!

MRS NOBLE } (*together*). Harold Headingford!
LUCY }

(HAROLD *advances to them. He is dressed in a sailor's jersey and trousers which do not quite meet. He frequently tries to cover the gap by violent tugs and hoists.*)

HAROLD. Yes, indeed, Mrs Noble, and sweet Lucy, it is I. We have not met since I ran away to sea ten years ago this very day.

LUCY. My brave Harold. (*She embraces* HAROLD *in a passionate, theatrical way.*)

HAROLD. My dear Lucy! So you still remember me.

LUCY. Yes, and I remember, too, the sacred vows of love we plighted in those happy childhood days.

HAROLD. I have been constant.

LUCY. And so have I. Now kindly fate has reunited us for ever.

(They embrace again.)

MRS NOBLE.   Alas that you should find us in such
a miserable state, for we are penniless and starving,
with scarce a roof above our heads.   *(She sobs.)*

PERCY ⎫
LUCY ⎭ *(together).*   Do not cry, dear mother.

PERCY.   I have acquainted Harold with the sad his-
tory of our family misfortunes.   Alas!   His own tale
is no less pitiful.   But stay.   Rest awhile on this bench
and he shall tell you.

(LUCY and MRS NOBLE sit.)

We have but scant provender for you, but shortly
Harold and I will search again.   *(He takes a chestnut
from his pocket.)*   Take this, mother, it was all I could
secure—a roasted chestnut.   I fear it is a little cold
by now.

HAROLD *(also taking a chestnut from his pocket).*
Sweet Lucy, I also procured one which you must have.

MRS NOBLE ⎫ *(together).* ⎰ No, no, I cannot eat it
LUCY   ⎭   ⎱ all.   You must share.

*(The chestnuts are divided.   HAROLD and PERCY sit at
the feet of the women.   They all nibble hungrily.)*

PERCY *(starting up; aside).*   Soft!   Who is the poor
fellow yonder?   He, too, looks cold and hungry.   He
shall share my frugal meal.   I cannot eat when I
behold such suffering.   *(He crosses to BOWLER and
awakens him.)*   Sir, sir, I cannot doubt but that you
are in some distress.   I, too, am penniless and starving,
but I can at least offer you the comfort of half of my
half-chestnut.

BOWLER.   Heaven bless you for your kind words.
It is true; I am starving.   Once I had wealth—no
matter how I got it—but I was foolish and gambled
my fortune away.   Your kindness gives me fresh hope.

(BOWLER *and* PERCY *eat and converse.*)

MRS NOBLE (*to* HAROLD). So your plight is even worse than ours? No roof to shelter you. Alas, that we should know such sorrow. (*She sobs.*)

LUCY. Do not cry, dear mother. Harold shall come home with us to our mean attic. I will gladly let him share my bed.

MRS NOBLE. Hush, hush, my child. (*Aside.*) She is so innocent.

BOWLER (*to* PERCY). And once I find this gentleman, I shall make him pay. I have a certain slip of paper that he will gladly buy for ten thousand pounds.

PERCY. Heavens! Is there so much money in the world?

BOWLER. You are young and money is a god to children. But hear me, my lad, an easy conscience and a contented heart are worth all the gold in the world.

PERCY. Thank you. Now I must go, but first tell me your name.

BOWLER. My name is Bowler. And yours?

PERCY. Percy Noble, son of the late Captain Noble.

BOWLER (*aside*). Merciful Heaven. Can this be possible?

PERCY. And yonder are my starving mother and sister whom I must rejoin. Good-bye, Mr Bowler, and may Heaven bless you. (*He rejoins the others.*) Come, let us go. Harold and I to the Opera House where we may perchance earn a copper or two by holding the horses' heads. You, my dear mother and sweet Lucy, go back to our mean attic in Cross Keys Street, and we will join you within the hour.

(MRS NOBLE *sobs.*)

PERCY
LUCY } (*together*). Do not cry, dear mother.

(They kiss and depart. HAROLD *and* PERCY *exit* L.
MRS NOBLE *and* LUCY *exit* R.)

BOWLER *(rising).* Poor, poor, poor people. How
my heart bleeds for them. How brave and kind they
are. *(He advances down stage.)* Now I am resolved.
That villainous thief, Silas Snaker, shall pay for this.
I will renew my weary search for him and force him
to pay me the money which I will then hand over to
Percy Noble. The vile and rascally Snaker must not,
shall not, rob these poor and innocent gentlefolk.

(There are cheers.)

(He looks off L.) But soft, do my eyes deceive me?
It cannot be . . . But yes it is—none other than
Snaker himself coming this way, doubtless from some
sumptuous banquet. Thank you, O Heaven, for thus
delivering the villain into my hands.

(Sinister music is played as SNAKER, *in astrakhan,
enters* L. *He carries a stick. There are boos.)*

A word with you, if you please.
    SNAKER. Out of my way, cur. I have no pity for
beggars.
    BOWLER. I do not beg. I demand.
    SNAKER *(raising his stick).* Insolent dog. Who are
you?
    BOWLER. My name is Bowler. I was once your
clerk.
    SNAKER *(aside).* That name strikes terror in my
heart. Bowler? Ah! Yes, I believe I did once
employ a fellow of that name. But I have no need
for clerks now. Here, take this shilling and let me
pass.
    BOWLER. No, no, my fine sir!
    SNAKER *(aside).* Foiled!

BOWLER. For three years I have searched for you high and low. Now fate has brought us together.

SNAKER. I do not understand you. Be brief or let me pass.

BOWLER. Noble! Ten thousand pounds! Receipt! Do those words strike any answering chord in your black heart? Aha, I see they do. I still have that receipt. Unless you pay me ten thousand pounds I will go straight to the police!

SNAKER (aside). Foiled again! Let me see this receipt. (Aside.) He may have lost it.

BOWLER. Ha! Ha! It is too precious to carry about. I have it in my lodgings, and you must come for it and bring the money with you.

SNAKER (aside). Curse him, he has me in his power. Yet I may still find a way to thwart him. Very well, I will visit you tomorrow.

BOWLER. Within the hour you must come or your vile secret will be with the police. I live in Cross Keys Street. My lodgings are but a mean attic, but you will find me waiting. Farewell, Silas Snaker, and on your peril, fail me not.

(BOWLER exits R.)

SNAKER. Foiled again.

(SNAKER exits L.)

CURTAIN

SCENE 3

SCENE: *The Attics in Cross Keys Street. The stage is divided into two attics, with a short length of party wall between them. The room* R. *belongs to* BOWLER *and the room* L. *to* MRS NOBLE. *Each room has a door and a window. In the room* R. *is a small camp-bed, table, chair and a cupboard. In the room* L. *a table and two chairs.*

When the CURTAIN *rises* MRS NOBLE *and* LUCY *are discovered sitting in the chairs.*

LUCY. Surely an hour has passed and Percy and Harold have not yet returned.

MRS NOBLE. Oh! Merciful Father! Protect my innocent children.

(BOWLER *enters his room* R.)

BOWLER. Back again to these miserable lodgings. How dark it is. (*He takes a box containing two matches, from his pocket.*) I have but two matches left, but what matter—(*lighting the candle*)—this poor candle must be both light and heat for me for I have no fuel at all.

LUCY. Do not cry, dear mother. See, the candle is going out.

MRS NOBLE. So much the better. Now you will not be able to see my tears.

BOWLER (*going to the cupboard*). What poor provisions have I left? Tonight I will eat all that is left, for surely Percy Noble will no longer let me starve once I have retrieved his family fortune.

LUCY (*aside*). Is there no way to end this misery? None but death!

BOWLER (*examining a bottle*). Ha, ha! One last bottle of honest ale remains. This shall warm me and cheer me up for my encounter with the rascally Snaker. A few dry crusts and this piece of raw meat I snatched from a dog last week, these must perforce be my repast. (*He sits and proceeds to roast the meat over the candle.*)

MRS NOBLE (*aside*). If Percy had only Lucy to support, they might live. Why should I prolong my life merely to shorten theirs?

BOWLER (*rising and examining the party wall*). This room grows draughtier than ever. What can it be? Why, yes, there are great chinks in the wall here. Heaven grant that I may soon be free of the place and live once more in the comfort I used to know. A new family moved in next door some days ago. I have not seen them. I wonder who they are? (*He resumes his meal.*)

LUCY (*aside*). There is but one solution: I must die. When I am gone there will be one less mouth to feed. My duty is plain: I must think of my mother. My sacrifice is for her alone.

MRS NOBLE (*aside*). In this room there is some charcoal. (*She rises.*) But is there enough to bestow on me an easy death?

(MRS NOBLE *exits.*)

LUCY. What is mother doing? (*She looks through the door.*) She is lighting the pan of charcoal on which we prepare our food. Ah! A thought! Could I induce her to leave me alone, the deadly fumes of the fuel would soon bestow on me an easy death.

(MRS NOBLE *enters.*)

MRS NOBLE (*aside*). It is there; now while I have the courage of despair.

BOWLER. Snaker should soon be here. What is the time, I wonder?

(*A church clock strikes ten very erratically.*)

Ha!   Ten o'clock.

(*The clock strikes once more.*)

Eleven o'clock.   He will be here anon I have no doubt.

LUCY.   Dear mother, I have just thought of a friend,
a working girl, from whom I might beg a crust.

MRS NOBLE.   Go then, my child—go at once.

LUCY.   I fear to go alone.   Come with me and
wait at the corner of the street till I come out.

MRS NOBLE (*aside*).   When she is out of sight I can
return and accomplish my purpose.

LUCY (*aside*).   I will leave her and come back
quickly by another way to accomplish my purpose.

MRS NOBLE.   Come, Lucy.   (*She sobs.*)

LUCY (*as they go to the door*).   Do not cry, dear
mother.

(MRS NOBLE *and* LUCY *exit.*)

BOWLER (*draining the bottle*).   Gone, all is gone.
But now I must make ready for my guest.   Ha!   Ha!
(*He clears the table.*)

(*Horses' hooves are heard off.*)

He comes!   I hear his carriage below.   The receipt!
(*He opens the cupboard.*)   Yes, safely here.   (*He puts
it in his pocket.*)   Now I am ready to bargain with this
vile monster.

(*Music is heard as* SNAKER *enters* R.)

SNAKER.   Ah! ha!   So this is your abode?   (*Aside.*)
This place fills me with horror and foreboding.   I
must get the receipt and go quickly.   Where is the
receipt you spoke of?

BOWLER. Not so fast. Where is the money I also spoke of?

SNAKER. I have left it below guarded by my coachman. You shall have it when you have given me the receipt—*if* you have got the receipt, which I greatly doubt.

BOWLER. Make no mistake, the receipt is here in my pocket.

SNAKER. You lie.

BOWLER (*producing the receipt*). There! Vile wretch. It is you who lie.

SNAKER (*chasing* BOWLER *round the table*). Give it to me. Curse you, curse you, curse you.

BOWLER. Not so fast. Bring me the money and it is yours.

SNAKER (*producing a pistol*). Give it to me at once, or I'll blow your brains out.

BOWLER. So that is your calculation.

SNAKER. Now I have you in my power. Ha! ha! ha! I am one too many for you.

BOWLER (*producing two pistols from under the bed*). And I am one too many for you. I defy you, Silas Snaker.

(*There are cheers.*)

SNAKER (*dropping the pistol; aside*). Damnation! Foiled again. Curse him, I am at his mercy. Ha! ha! ha! I was merely playing. I hope my little joke didn't upset you.

BOWLER. A joke you say? Very well, you shall pay for your joke. It will cost you an extra thousand pounds. Unless you bring to me within fifteen minutes the sum of eleven thousand pounds I shall go straight to the police.

SNAKER. Mercy! Mercy! I shall be ruined.

BOWLER. Perhaps you would rather be hanged?

SNAKER. No! no! Anything but that. Give me time to pay. Here, take my purse and I will visit you **again** next week.

BOWLER. Your purse is too small for my liking. Go, fetch the full amount within fifteen minutes or I will expose your villainy to the whole world. Go!

SNAKER (*going to the door and turning*). Foiled again.

(SNAKER *exits. There are boos.*)

BOWLER. So! Now I can take my ease for a few minutes. (*He sits.*)

(LUCY *enters* L.)

LUCY. I took a short cut and ran home. Now I am alone the fumes of charcoal shall fill this little room and send me to sleep for ever. I must fetch the pan. (*She exits.*)

BOWLER. Ah, how I look forward to relieving the widow and her fatherless children.

(MRS NOBLE *enters* L.)

MRS NOBLE. Poor Lucy. I dared not look back at her as we parted for ever. Despair hastened my steps. My poor, innocent children. I have given you all I had, and now I hope my wretched life will serve you in your terrible need.

BOWLER (*sniffing*). I smell charcoal, burning charcoal. (*He rises.*) Where can it be coming from? I have a queer feeling in my head. Let me lie down awhile. (*He lies on the bed.*)

(LUCY *enters* L. *with a charcoal brazier.*)

LUCY. The moment has arrived.

MRS NOBLE (*seeing her*). Lucy!

LUCY. Mother!

MRS NOBLE. My child, what is this? For what purpose are you here?

LUCY. You, too, mother? Like me, you wished to die?

MRS NOBLE. No! no! You shall not die! My darling child, you are too young. Life is before you —hope—happiness. (*She sobs.*)

LUCY. Do not cry, dear mother. Is it not better to die like this than by either grief or hunger?

MRS NOBLE (*falling into a chair*). Already my senses fail me. Lucy, my child, live, live!

LUCY. No! No, dear mother, let us die together. First I must lock the door. (*She locks the door and then kneels beside her mother.*) Let us pray together for those whom we leave. Can you hear me, mother?

BOWLER. Oh! I feel so ill. Why does my brain reel so; why does my head throb? (*He groans.*)

(*There is a knocking on the door L. PERCY and HAROLD are outside.*)

PERCY (*off*). The door is locked, Harold. What can it mean? Mother, Lucy, open the door. It is I, Percy. What is wrong? Mother, we have food for you. Open! Open!

(*LUCY falls prostrate.*)

Harold, help me to burst open the door.

(*HAROLD and PERCY burst open the door and enter.*)

Woe is me! What is this? They have committed suicide.

(*PERCY rushes to MRS NOBLE and HAROLD to LUCY. They take out handkerchiefs and fan the women vigorously.*)

BOWLER (*rising*). I cannot breathe. Oh! Heaven, why do you torture me thus. I am dying—dying within a moment of triumph. (*He chokes.*) I am suffocating. What can I do? I cannot see. Oh! how my head spins.

(MRS NOBLE *and* LUCY *revive.*)

PERCY. There, there, dear mother, all is well. The fresh air has revived you. Thank Heaven we were in time.

MRS NOBLE. My brave boy, you have rescued us from the grave. I had planned it all for your sake.

BOWLER. Justice of Heaven! I am strangling— (*tearing off his collar*)—and Snaker will be here at any moment. If he finds me thus he will rob me of my receipt just as he robbed that poor old sailor. I know him of old. I must get help. (*He knocks on the party wall.*) Help, help, good neighbours.

(SNAKER *enters* R. *carrying a portmanteau.* BOWLER *falls unconscious.*)

PERCY. What was that? I heard a muffled cry for help.

HAROLD. And so did I. It seemed to come from the next room.

LUCY. Let us go and see if we can render assistance.

(*They all exit.*)

SNAKER. Ah, ha! So he is drunk. Now I have him in my power. But how stifling it is in here. I must open the window or I shall choke. (*He opens the window.*) Poor fool, how he has played into my hands. (*He kicks* BOWLER.) Take that, and that, and that. Now for the receipt. Which pocket did he use? (*He kneels by* BOWLER.)

(MRS NOBLE, LUCY, PERCY *and* HAROLD *enter* R.)

PERCY. Pardon us, sir, but we heard a cry for help and have come to render assistance.

SNAKER (*rising; aside*). Foiled again! Ah, my friends, that is good of you, but there is nothing you can do. My friend has merely swooned, but I am a doctor and I will take care of him myself. Thank you most kindly. Good night!

HAROLD. But is there nothing we can do? He looks so ill and there is blood on his forehead.

SNAKER (*aside*). Curse it, that is where I kicked him. No, no, my friends, you may safely leave him to me. Good night!

MRS NOBLE. Nay, I will fetch some water for his poor bruised lips.

SNAKER (*aside*). Curse it! My second kick. I can attend to all. Good night.

LUCY. Here, take my handkerchief to bind his bloody neck.

MRS NOBLE. Hush, hush, my child. (*Aside.*) She is so innocent.

(BOWLER *revives*.)

BOWLER (*sitting up*). Where am I?

ALL. Ah! He is coming to.

SNAKER. And so, my friends, I bid you good night. (*He starts to shepherd them out.*)

BOWLER (*rising*). Stay! Do not go. And, most important, do not let him go. He is a thief, nay, little better than a murderer.

(*There are cheers.*)

SNAKER (*aside*). Foiled again!

PERCY. Why! Mr. Bowler!

BOWLER. By all that's wonderful—Percy Noble.

SNAKER (*aside*). Noble! That name again. I fear the worst is about to befall me.

PERCY. Let me introduce my mother and sister, Lucy. This is a poor friend whom I met tonight.

(*They all bow.*)

BOWLER (*aside*). How charming and gracious the old lady is. I believe I love her.

MRS NOBLE (*aside*). How unhappy he looks. Yet how brave and noble. I believe I love him.

BOWLER. Mrs Noble, dear madam. As you and yours have so gallantly come to my aid, now may I succour you and relieve you of your cares.

MRS. NOBLE (*aside*). What *can* he mean? This is so sudden.

BOWLER. Five years ago this very night your gallant husband met with sudden but natural death.

LUCY ⎱
PERCY ⎰ (*together*). Do not cry, dear mother.

BOWLER. Shortly before this cruel fate overtook him, he entrusted to Silas Snaker, a banker, ten bags of golden sovereigns. I was there, I saw it all.

LUCY ⎫
PERCY ⎬ (*together*). You.
MRS NOBLE ⎭

BOWLER. Yes. I must confess, to my shame, that I helped the villain, Snaker, to embezzle the money. But that is past. I am reformed—won back to virtue by the kindliness of your noble son and the gentleness of your lovely face. I am ready to make amends with my life. Nay, more, I am about to restore your husband's savings into your hands.

MRS NOBLE. Sir, I am amazed at what you tell us. How can this be?

BOWLER (*pointing to* SNAKER). There stands the monstrous villain, Silas Snaker.

LUCY ⎫
PERCY ⎬ (*together*). Vile, ignoble creature!
MRS NOBLE ⎭

(*There are boos and hisses.*)

SNAKER (*aside*). Damnation and fury. Can I find a way out? My good friends, I have let this go too far and I must apologize. As I told you a few moments ago, I am a doctor, and this is my patient. So much is true. (*He points to the portmanteau.*) There is my professional bag. But when I said he swooned, I lied, merely to save your feelings. He was in a fit. He is subject to fits, dreadful fits in which he bites his lips and bangs his head. He is dangerous. In fact, my good friends, he is a lunatic, and I have traced him here to take him back to Colney Hatch. Now leave us at once while you are safe.

(*They all back to the door with suitable exclamations of horror.*)

BOWLER. Stop! Do not believe this lying rogue. I have proof of my story.

SNAKER (*aside*). The receipt! Foiled again!

BOWLER (*taking the receipt from his pocket*). Here is the receipt signed by his own hand, and there in the bag is the money he stole.

PERCY (*examining both*). Mother, it is true! We are rich again.

MRS NOBLE. Oh! Happy circumstance. Mr Bowler, how can I ever express my thanks? (*She offers her hand to* BOWLER.) *Cross & stay*

(BOWLER *kisses her hand.*)

PERCY (*to* SNAKER). And you, miserable miscreant, have you nothing to say before we send for the police?

SNAKER. Alas, what can I say? I am undone, exposed, unmasked—and utterly foiled.

PERCY. Is there not one thing in his favour?

SNAKER. Nothing save this. All I have done has been because of love—love of my sweet, innocent and motherless daughter. For her alone I desired riches and high degree. For her alone I have striven these last five weary years.　Sweet, darling Alice, I can see her now.　(*He sobs.*)

LUCY (*to* SNAKER; *absent-mindedly*).　Do not cry dear mother.

MRS NOBLE.　My heart is touched.　I have seen too much of suffering.　Do not send him to gaol.　Let him go.

BOWLER.　My sweet angel, your forgiving heart is a shining example to us all.

PERCY.　Be it so.　Snaker, you may thank my mother for this generous clemency.　Let her noble sacrifice be an example to you.　Mend your ways, cleanse your heart, resolve to follow the path of virtue —and never darken my doors again.

SNAKER.　I am resolved.　Henceforward I shall be an honourable and humble man.　Nor pleasures nor palaces shall ever tempt me more.

ALL.　Amen.

(SNAKER *exits to soft music.*)

HAROLD.　And now, Lucy, I claim your hand.

BOWLER.　And I, sweet madam, humbly sue for yours.

MRS NOBLE
LUCY
} (*together*). { We have learned the value of poverty.　It opens the heart.

PERCY (*coming to the front of the stage and addressing the audience*).　Is this true?　Have the sufferings we have depicted opened your hearts and caused a sympathetic tear to fill your eyes?　If so, extend to us your hands.

MRS NOBLE (*to the audience*).　No, not to us.　But when you leave this place, as you go home, should you see some poor creatures, extend your hands to them and Heaven will shower blessings in your way.

CURTAIN

TABLEAU

PRODUCTION NOTES

Hiss the Villain! is modelled very closely to the type of melodrama which was immensely popular in the 1850's. It should be played with great earnestness and sincerity, and the actors must never move outside their characters for the sake of a laugh. The Victorian audience played almost as large a part in the performance as the actors themselves, sharing very enthusiastically in the emotions of the hero and heroine. It is, therefore, essential to a really good performance to get your audience entering whole-heartedly into the fun. In the original performance a claque was enlisted. They attended several rehearsals and soon became proficient in hissing and cheering at appropriate moments. On the night of the performance the audience quickly " cottoned-on " and the play went with a tremendous swing.

A good deal of extra fun can be devised with the snow in Scene 2 by selecting special moments and places for it to fall. For instance, a brief shower of scarlet snow at BOWLER'S line " How my heart bleeds for them " always brings the house down. Again an apparently involuntary snowfall in the middle of Scene 3 is very successful!

LUCY'S oft-repeated " Do not cry, dear mother," is more pointed if she produces each time a tiny handkerchief, and especially if they are all fresh handkerchiefs produced from unexpected quarters of her costume.

The costumes themselves present little difficulty. SNAKER has a frock coat; PERCY, a much-too-small Norfolk suit; and the ladies are shabbily genteel in long skirts and leg-o'-mutton sleeves.

Music can help the atmosphere immensely, especially the sentimental piece " Hearts and Flowers," played softly in pathetic moments. A small orchestra is best, of course, but failing that, a piano and violin, or even a gramophone, would be useful.

FURNITURE AND PROPERTY LIST

SCENE 1

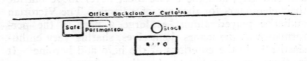

Office Backcloth or Curtains

Safe Portmanteau Stool

B/FO

Desk
Stool
Safe. *In it:* six bags of gold
Portmanteau

Personal:—

NOBLE: receipt, pistol

SCENE 2

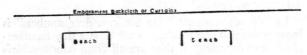

Embankment Backcloth or Curtains

Bench Bench

Two benches
Personal:—

LUCY: handkerchiefs
PERCY: chestnut
HAROLD: chestnut
SNAKER: stick

24

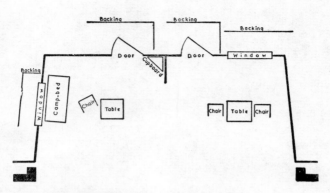

MRS NOBLE'S Room: —
    Table. *On it:* stub of candle (*lit*)
    Two chairs
    In the door: key

BOWLER'S Room: —
    Camp-bed. *Under it:* two pistols
    Table. *On it:* candle
    Chair
    Cupboard. *In it:* receipt, bottle of beer, crusts, piece
    of raw meat

Off L.: —
    Charcoal burner (LUCY)

Personal:—
    BOWLER: box with two matches
    SNAKER: pistol, portmanteau with money bags
    PERCY: handkerchief
    HAROLD: handkerchief

MADE AND PRINTED IN GREAT BRITAIN BY
LATIMER TREND AND CO. LTD, PLYMOUTH
MADE IN ENGLAND

MADE AND PRINTED IN GREAT BRITAIN BY
LATIMER TREND AND CO. LTD, PLYMOUTH
MADE IN ENGLAND